The Magical "I AM" Affirmation Bedtime Story

AF104583

The Magical "I AM" Affirmation Bedtime Story
Copyright © 2021 by Amy Petsalis

All rights reserved. No part of this publication may be reproduced, distributed, or transmitted in any form or by any means, including photocopying, recording, or other electronic or mechanical methods, without the prior written permission of the author, except in the case of brief quotations embodied in critical reviews and certain other non-commercial uses permitted by copyright law.

Tellwell Talent
www.tellwell.ca

ISBN
978-0-2288-4950-6 (Hardcover)
978-0-2288-4949-0 (Paperback)
978-0-2288-4951-3 (eBook)

MY DAUGHTER WAS MY INSPIRATION BEHIND THIS BOOK.
BEING A MOTHER, I WANTED TO START TEACHING MY DAUGHTER THE WONDERFUL PRACTICES THAT I USE IN MY OWN LIFE FOR MYSELF EACH DAY.
OUR BEDTIME ROUTINE IS A VERY SPECIAL TIME OF DAY WHEN WE CAN SAY A PRAYER AND AFFIRM ALL THAT WE ARE.
I WANTED TO CREATE THIS FOR CHILDREN EVERYWHERE IN THE WORLD, SO THEY CAN BE REMINDED HOW SPECIAL THEY TRULY ARE AND FALL ASLEEP IN HIGH VIBRATION, APPRECIATION AND IN ALIGNMENT WITH THEIR HEART.
-Amy

DEAR LITTLE CREATOR,
DREAM AND MAKE YOUR MAGIC COME ALIVE BY BEING THE POWERFUL PERSON THAT YOU ARE. YOU ARE SPECIAL AND UNIQUE FOR BEING YOU AND ONLY YOU.
FILL YOUR HEART WITH LOVE AND JOY EVERY NIGHT BEFORE YOU SLEEP, AND WAKE UP TO THE BIRDS SINGING TO ENJOY ANOTHER MAGICAL DAY.

-AMY

Now it is time to tell your own story..

I AM STRONG because...

I AM BRAVE because...

I AM BEAUTIFUL because...

I AM BLESSED because...

I AM KIND because...

I AM LOYAL because...

I AM WORTHY because...

I AM CREATIVE because...

I AM GRATEFUL because...

I AM LOVE because...

SWEET DREAMS, LITTLE ONE...

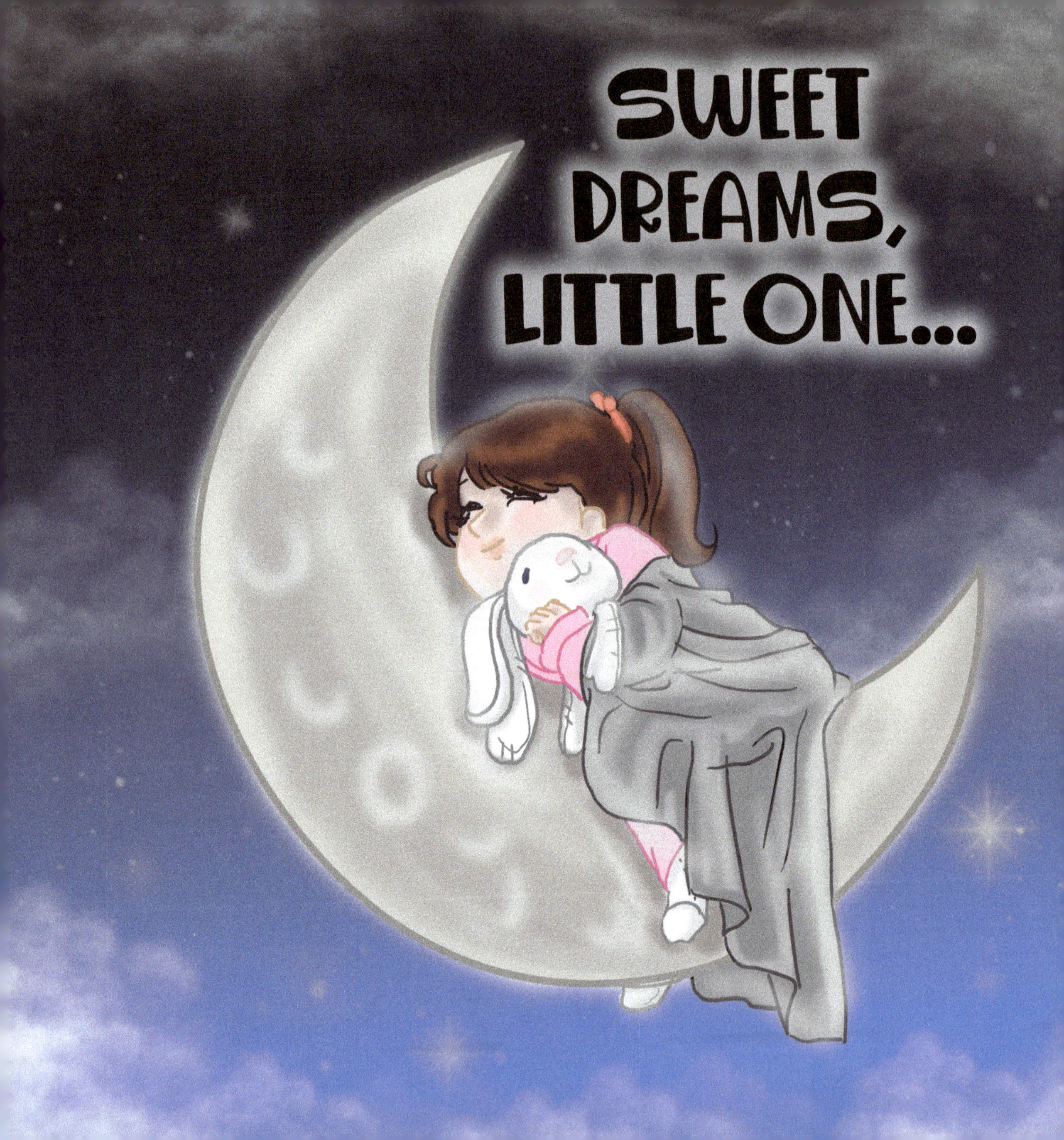

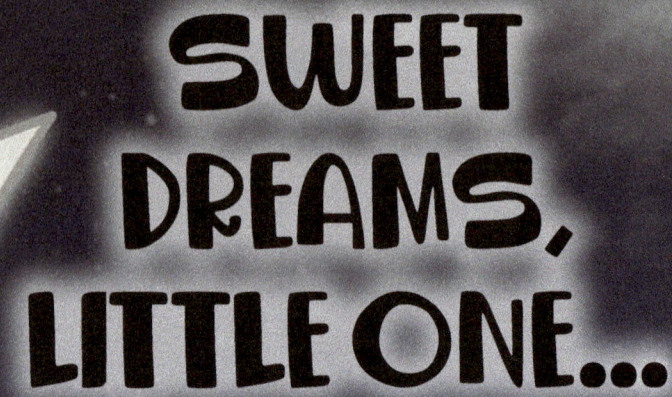

Author
Amy Petsalis

UNCENSORED & REAL

www.uncensoredandreal.net

Illustrator
Jenny Lyn Edaño Young

www.ingramcontent.com/pod-product-compliance
Lightning Source LLC
LaVergne TN
LVHW072016060526
838200LV00059B/4685